A Jazz-Inspired Christmas

8 Sophisticated Solo Piano Arrangements

Arranged by Craig Curry

This is the Christmas book I've always wanted to write. I'm excited to share these fresh-sounding, jazz-inspired piano arrangements with you, and I hope you will be excited in turn to share them in your church services, Christmas programs, concerts, and recitals. Enclosed is a CD that contains recordings of all of the pieces, as well as optional bass and drum parts for six of the arrangements, provided in PDF format. Chord symbols are included on the bass parts for those who might like to add guitar or other instruments. May you have an especially wonderful Christmas season, and may this book add to your enjoyment!

	Page	CD Track
The First Noel	14	3
Go, Tell It on the Mountain	36	8
God Rest Ye Merry, Gentlemen	26	6
Jingle Bells	9	2
O Little Town of Bethlehem	18	4
Silent Night	32	7
Sing We Now of Christmas	2	1
What Child Is This?	22	5

Alfred Music Publishing Co., Inc.
P.O. Box 10003
Van Nuys, CA 91410-0003
alfred.com

Copyright © MMXI by Alfred Music Publishing Co., Inc.
All rights reserved. Printed in USA.

No part of this book shall be reproduced, arranged, adapted, recorded, publicly performed, stored in a retrieval system, or transmitted by any means without written permission from the publisher. In order to comply with copyright laws, please apply for such written permission and/or license by contacting the publisher at alfred.com/permissions.
ISBN-10: 0-7390-8141-1
ISBN-13: 978-0-7390-8141-9

Cover Photos
Snowflakes: © istockphoto / wbs24

Sing We Now of Christmas

Traditional
Arr. Craig Curry

(Approx. Performance Time – 4:00)

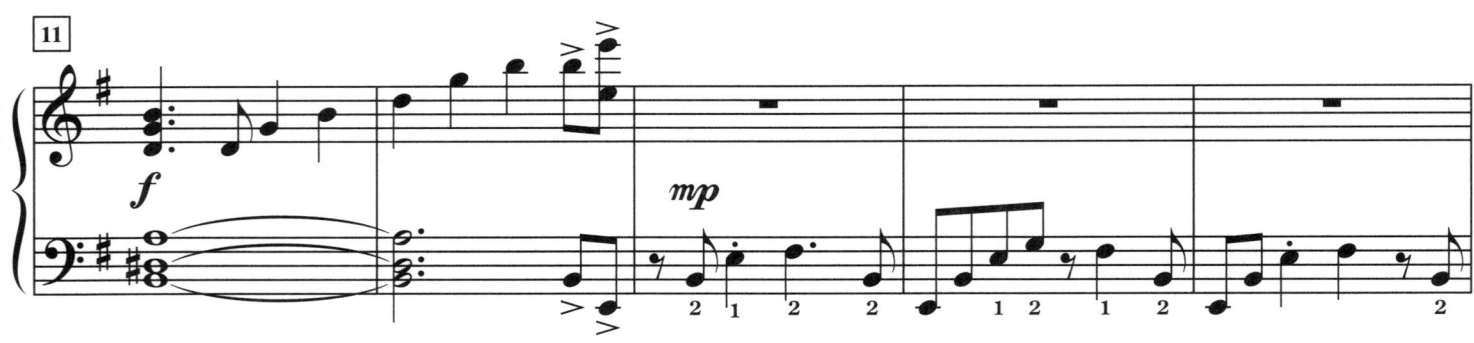

Jingle Bells

Traditional
Arr. Craig Curry

THE FIRST NOEL

(Approx. Performance Time – 3:30)

Traditional
Arr. Craig Curry

18

(Approx. Performance Time – 4:30)

O LITTLE TOWN OF BETHLEHEM

Lewis Radner
Arr. Craig Curry

(Approx. Performance Time – 4:30)

WHAT CHILD IS THIS?

Traditional
Arr. Craig Curry

God Rest Ye Merry, Gentlemen

Traditional
Arr. Craig Curry

Silent Night

(Approx. Performance Time – 3:30)

Franz Grüber
Arr. Craig Curry

Slow blues (♩. = 72)

34

36

(Approx. Performance Time – 3:00)

Go, Tell It on the Mountain

Traditional
Arr. Craig Curry